A CLIMBER'S MEMOIR

Charles R. Berry

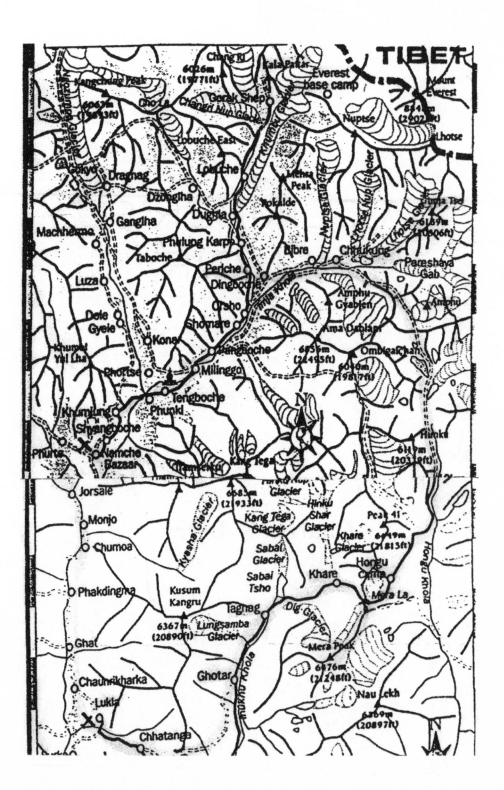

INTRODUCTION

This story is being written for my great grand-children, of whom I hope to meet several before my time passes.

I was always interested in my own great grandparents, and wished that I had something besides just a picture to give me insight into who they were and what they were like.

In addition, this tale will give you a glimpse of life in a remote part of the world where I was climbing one of the big mountains.

I hope you enjoy this true story, which was written from my journal after I returned home to Connecticut.

I am dedicating this book to me wife, Kathie, who for 57 years - and counting - has always encouraged me in my quest of climbing the big mountains. Without her enthusiasm this story would not have been possible.

September 2012

PROLOGUE

In the fall of 2004 when I was 69 years old, I was part of a 7 person team climbing 2 peaks in the Khumbu region of Nepal, just south of Everest, Lhotse, Nuptse and Makalu. Our goal was to summit Mera Peak and then to climb Island Peak.

This was a commercial trip with each of us paying $3,700 to be part of the climb. My climbing friend for the last 15 years, David Putnam, and I had been talking about this climb for several years as we thought it had all the elements that we were looking for in terms of challenge and exposure to a remote culture.

The leader of the climb was Adrian Ballinger, founder of Alpenglow Expeditions and his assistant was Jaime from Ecuador. We had checked Adrian's references and he had been given great reviews. The reason we liked the trip was that it immediately went off into very remote areas as opposed to the standard trek to Everest base camp with a climb of Island Peak thrown in.

September 19
Nirvana Garden Hotel
Thamel, Kathmandu, Nepal

David and I meet the rest of the group in Kathmandu in the late afternoon. We meet in the garden of the guest house with Adrian and the other 5. You will get to know them as I write about the next couple of weeks. Suffice to say on that fall afternoon we discuss logistics and what we are expecting over the next couple of weeks. We talk about our goals and our anxieties.

My goal is to summit and my anxiety is my age.

Adrian talks about what is going to happen over the next few days and then we go off for a nice dinner – the last fancy sit down meal we will have for the next three weeks.

September 20
Bom
10,789 feet

We are up early in the morning, have a quick breakfast at 5:30 and then get into a van with

all our gear for a rush to the Kathmandu airport. We have a big load and there is the normal hubbub of a Third World terminal with everyone yelling in Nepali as well as English and assorted other tongues.

We are loaded into a plane, all our gear piled into the front as well as into the back and off we go our little band of 9. We take off at 7:15 for Lukla and at 8:00 just before landing the plane turns and goes back to Kathmandu. After a 45 minute wait, we take off again.

David and I are seated in the front of the cabin and shortly before reaching Lukla we notice that the pilot is reading a newspaper. It is slightly disconcerting but this time we do land.

The landing strip at Lukla is cut into the side of a mountain so you land by flying uphill until you stop. Frequently planes don't stop, so there is plane wreckage scattered at the side of the only runway.

Our porters are waiting for us at a tea house in Lukla and they take the loads that came up with us in the plane. The balance of our stuff – food, tents, and all of the other miscellaneous gear a climb needs for three weeks

before resupply – has been sent ahead and our porters have already begun taking it to our first camp.

Our Nepali staff is made up of porters who carry loads of supplies and several climbing Sherpas. The Sherpas are Nepalese who are originally from Tibet. Several centuries ago they migrated over the Himalayas and settled in the Khumbu region. Our chief Sherpa is Nima. He is the sirdar, meaning that he is in charge of all of the Nepalese. He oversees the porters, organizing their loads as well as paying them at the end of the climb. In addition, he selects our camp sites each day and works with Adrian in ensuring that the overall climb goes smoothly. Our other Sherpas are Pemba and Endow, who assist Nima.

At the small tea house we have a quiet meal at 12 o'clock – everyone is subdued – and at 1 o'clock we are on the trail.

We head southeast, whereas everyone heading to Everest base camp goes north, so we are alone. It seems steep right from the start. It is raining so we are wet and it is slippery. Each person seems to be quiet and walking alone. It is a short afternoon, but all

our gear is wet. By 5 o'clock, we have stopped and are in our tents. David and I sort our gear and by 6:00 the rain has stopped and we have dinner – a nice soup, Dalbat, rice, gravy, chicken, fruit salad, and dessert.

My blood concentration level in the morning is 98-64 and in the evening it is down to 94-68. Those are good readings and I feel strong. Blood concentration levels are important as they are a measure of how well you are acclimatizing. The altitude is 10789.

September 21
Base of Zair La
13,154 feet

We go past Chhatanga – basically no village, no nothing. We had bed tea at 6:00 AM and were packed and ready to go at 7:00 when breakfast was served – coffee, oatmeal, eggs fried over and all you can eat. We left camp at 8:00 with porters ahead and porters behind us. The trail was all up, and after a short day we were at camp by 11:30.

The altitude is 13,154, the temperature is 55. We arrived at camp in a mist that turned to rain, sometimes soft and then sometimes

hard. Lunch was at 12:30 – soup, cheese, tuna, and several cups of tea.

Great meals. We eat our meals in a tent with a table down the middle and 5 seats on each side. Kihlar the cook, or cook boy, a young 16 year old in a red flannel shirt, brings the food to one end of the tent and we pass it down.

I led most of the morning at an easy pace that everyone seemed to like. After lunch at the table – our meeting place – Adrian talked about altitude sickness, the symptoms and the cure. I will stay on Diamox 250 mg at breakfast, 250 mg at dinner. I am drinking lots of fluids and so far my urine is copious and clear.

At night I drink a liter of fluid and pass at least that much during the night. During the day I drink at least 2 liters.

My heart rate is 68, and my blood concentration is at 85. I will try to get it higher. Adrian and I compete to see who has the best oxygen concentration level and so far we are close. Good for me.

Some Germans just came down from Zair La. They had started from Lukla, gone up to

Chungkung, gone over the Amphu Lapcha and attempted Mera. They could not summit because there was too much snow. I think they got to the central summit.

No time yet to dry clothes, so everything stays wet. So far I feel very good. The altimeter is a huge hit with everyone asking "how high, how high". I sure hope that the batteries don't give out. Some where my Ritz-Carlton hat got lost. I'll probably next see it on the head of a Nepali in Kathmandu.

September 22
Thulikara
13,838 feet

Up at 5:45, I took a sleeping pill last night but I still didn't sleep very well. I have always considered this a key day for we go over the Zair-La at 15,200 feet. This is very high for so early in our climb, with so little acclimatizing. Hence, my nervousness.

Of course, another reason I didn't sleep well is that I passed a liter and a half into the pee bottle during the night and that takes time!

Bed tea at 6:00 am, break down our tent and pack our gear. This we can now do pretty fast since in the evening we only roll out our sleeping bag, have a stuff sack with toothbrush , powder for feet and sleep in our first layer. We wash our face in the hot water that comes by our tent at 6:20 and by 7:00 we are packed and ready to eat breakfast.

While we eat in the meal tent the porters are knocking down the tents, and making up their loads. Therefore by the time we finish eating and visit the "green tent", the toilet, the porters are also ready to go. Today we left camp at 7:26.

I led the whole way to the Zair-La, very slow and steady.

The porters climb differently. They go fast with the heavy load, then rest for a while, then start up fast again. The net result is that you see the same porters all day long, they pass you, you pass them, etc. I just keep going and don't stop except when I hear "Porter coming" and then I get off to the side of the trail and let them pass.

After 1½ hours of slow and steady climbing we were there. It was a steady steep, but not

as hard as I expected. Once there, we waited ½ hour for the rest of the team with Lynette bringing up the rear, with Nima at her side. The real pass is another 800 feet higher, so we pushed off again slow and steady and wow! Here we are.

I feel very good with a very slight headache for just a few minutes.

The team looks strong. Gay, Dan, Lissa, David, Tim and I are all similar in speed although Lissa likes to go faster.

All my systems are good, with the camel-back being terrific. Every now and then I suck on it and seem to drink a liter or more in the morning on the fly. I am very happy with my conditioning; everything is good except I seem to have slight head congestion.

The mountains are majestic, but it is raining intermittently so not only is a lot of stuff wet and not drying but you can't see much when you do look up since the clouds are low. Oh well.

Most of the time I am wearing the light poly bottoms, khaki shorts, heavy poly top and the black Helly Hansen when weather or

rain dictate. The first big hurdle is over and I am very, very pleased with the result.

It is now 11:30 and we are greeted with hot lemonade.

Oh yes, when we arrived here in this large camp site there were Russians here as well. We have not seen them before so they must be moving at a different pace. I can't figure the Russians out. They must have had a rest day today, since they didn't pass us and there is no place to camp above us after the Zair-La. It is strange to have a rest day so early in an expedition.

The Maoists are here too with a red flag in the middle of the village. There are three huts that comprise the village that is called Thulikharka. The altitude is 13,838.

September 23
Khotar
12,285 feet

Today we hiked to the village of Khotar, altitude 12,285. We arrived at our camp at 3:10 after leaving Thulikharka at 8:00. Along the way we stopped 1½ hours for lunch.

Where we stopped for lunch was alongside a lovely stream that was flowing very rapidly. We all gathered on a small patch of grass, maybe 20 feet by 30 feet, and had the lunch that Kihlar made for us. Like every day, Kihlar made a hot soup and then some cheese sandwiches. We are not going to starve on this climb if it continues like this.

Today was a wet, wet slog over slippery rocks all up and down. If we were not on rocks then we were on mud, yes real mud that grabbed our boots and was more slippery than the rocks. Very unpleasant. All day long, I saw nothing but 6 feet in front of me and 2 feet on either side of the trail. Most of the day it was raining. Sometimes it was just drizzling and when it wasn't doing either of those things, the clouds were just very low. No sight-seeing since you had to concentrate on foot placement all the time.

We had some very hairy crossing of raging rivers, sometimes using logs and sometimes jumping, well maybe leaping, from boulder to boulder. Fortunately none of us fell in.

The altitude change during the day included lots of steep ups and then lots of steep downs. So I think you get the idea that it was a

tough day when you added in the rain and the slippery conditions.

Endow Sherpa led a group of us who were the most consistent in moving along the trail and who were moving at a good pace and that included Lissa, Tim, Gay, David and me. My training is really paying off as I feel very good and healthy and comfortable when moving with the fastest of our team. I sweated and got wet from the rain.

Today I wore light poly bottoms, shorts, red heavy poly top – sometimes zipped sometimes not – and the black Helly Hansen wind breaker when it rained.

Today, we were in Maoist territory, with their blue symbols painted on rocks from time to time. I can't figure who the symbols are meant for since we never see anyone, but nonetheless our sirdar Nima has told us that if we are asked by anyone we are to say "we are Australian."

The food continues to be fantastic. This is far and away the best led and best organized climb I have ever been on. We are a party of 30/35 – including the cooks, cook's helpers, porters, Sherpa's, etc.

David and I get up around 5:45, so that we are all dressed, and are putting our gear in our packs by the time the cook boy comes by at 6:00 and at our tent door says " Bed Tea." That means he is standing right outside our tent with a tray of cups, hot water, instant coffee, instant hot chocolate, warm milk and cookies. What a way to start the day!

Last night, I took two Sudafed to ward off a possible cold that David has, and I took another 2 this morning.

As I write this, I have just gotten into my stuff sack #1, a day earlier than I had planned in order to get dry socks and underwear. In organizing my pack I have several stuff sacks labeled 1 through 4, each with underwear and socks that are to be opened at the first of each week. Since it has been raining so much nothing has had a chance to dry out.

David keeps saying "we should have waited another week before we started in order to miss the end of the monsoon season." My poly bottoms are damp but if I put them between my sleeping bag and my pad they should be dry by morning – hopefully. Right now, they are hanging on an interior clothes line.

I hope to use the satellite telephone after Mera. So far, I am performing up to my highest expectations – hope it lasts. And speaking of hopes, I hope it stops raining soon so that we can dry things out.

Khotar is a real village. It was destroyed by a huge flood 5 years ago that came down the valley. The valley which is about 400 yards wide was wiped cleaned of everything in the water's path up to a level about 100 feet above the current water level. It happened when a glacial moraine at the end of a lake about 10 miles upstream broke up suddenly and all of the impounded water was let loose to cascade down the narrow river valley. It destroyed everything in its path.

Now 6 structures have been built including a saw mill. The saw mill is a two person deal. It works like this. A log is rolled along the ground until one end is over a 7 foot deep hole, and then a person gets in the hole and grabs one end of the saw. The other wood cutter gets above that end of the log on a platform, grabs the other end of the saw and they start pulling the saw back and forth. And that is how they cut a tree into boards. You don't want to be the guy in the hole!

September 24
Tangnag
14,600 feet

We left Khotar at 7:55 am with all of us right together. It seemed quite orderly and everyone seemed fine. Well maybe some of the team seemed a little weary, but on balance OK.

This is Maoist territory.

Traveling on about the same schedule as us are the Russians, about 6 climbers and their support team. They left after us this morning but they go fast and as they passed me they asked "what did you give to the Maoist? We had to give them our guitar." I replied that we had given them nothing "We're Australians!" It seems to be the magic word and the Russians were quite surprised.

The trail runs right alongside the Hinku Khola with unbelievable signs of the lake breakout 5 years ago. I felt fine the whole day.

About 1 hour before we got to Tangnag, we visited a 1 monk monastery, located in a

cave built up above the trail. The monastery was small, maybe 20 feet by 20 feet, with an elaborate altar at the far end. I gave the yellow scarf that Pemba Sherpa in Boulder had given to Liz, to the monk for a blessing – along with 20 rupees. I went up to the altar area with the scarf laid over my hands and extended out in front of me. The monk sprinkled the scarf and me with rice and at the same time did a lot of good sounding mumbling. The scarf is now in the outside pocket of my day pack and it will go with me on Mera. I hope it helps.

Tangnag is the last village in the Hokhu Khola river valley. It is sited at the end of the valley about an hour or two below the lake that caused all the damage to the valley below. It is in a meadow probably ½ mile square and has 4 houses and a tea house.

As we walked into town, I notice a woman in a small field next to her house hoeing and digging up potatoes for dinner. She must be used to people passing through because she did not look up as we walked by.

A little further on, I encountered two young girls, maybe 6 and 8, laughing and giggling, just as happy as they could be and playing

with a toy they shared. On closer inspection the toy was a dead bird.

Our camp is next to a small stream that is flowing quite fast and the porters have already set up our tents by the time we arrive. They had not stopped at the monastery.

We have great views of Mera to our southeast and Kasum Konga to our northwest. In other words there are beautiful mountains wherever you look, that is, whenever the clouds clear. We don't have rain, just mist and chill. In the mornings we seem to have our nice weather and as the day wears on the clouds come in.

Today, we lost one porter. That seems to be normal since beyond Tagnag the real climbing begins and they get scared. Since they only are paid $3.00 per day I don't blame them. Especially when faced with the prospect of going over the Amphu Lapcha at 19,000 feet which is one of only two ways out once you get beyond Tagnag.

September 25
Tangnag
14,600 feet

This is a rest day. We sleep until 7:00 am and have breakfast at 7:30. At 8:00 a tin dish of hot water appears in front the tents and several of us decide to wash our hair and rid ourselves of some of the Nepali dirt we have picked up during the last week. Nothing like getting a little cleaner to lift the spirits.

Five more porters left camp during the night, so Nima is trying to find replacements. Obviously, in this remote part of the world he is going to have an impossible time, but he is trying. I gather he has found one. Not bad considering where we are. And of course, we don't need as many porters since we have eaten some of our supplies during the past week, making the loads lighter.

From 10 until 4 with a break for lunch we practice techniques we will use during the next week. Everyone is checked out on a crevice rescue system. The system works so that if someone on your rope falls into a crevice you can stabilize them while they work themselves up the rope and out. It

basically is moving up a rope with a prussic knot that you slide up above you and do the same with a foot loop. We also worked on moving on a fixed line with a jumar and/or a prussic knot.

Adrian is a very impressive young man. This is far and away the best prepared, organized, managed, and led trek or climb I have ever been on.

Consider the food and the food handling, always an important part of any climb. Kihlar, the cook and the cook boys are always washing their hands and the water they give us has always been boiled. And speaking of boiled water, it is always available so that we can keep our fluids up so as to acclimatize properly.

And the food is always great. Today for example, at breakfast we had oatmeal, followed by pineapple pancakes. At lunch, sitting on a small deck overlooking the brook, we had chicken broth with noodles, followed by chunk tuna, coleslaw, and finished off with a tomato pizza. But we need a lot of food since we are burning a lot of calories.

At 4 we started to organize our gear for the

summit push. David and I had put all of our climbing gear into one duffel that we had not touched until now. It had all our climbing stuff as well as extras that we would not need until later on. Of course as we opened the bag the first thing we found was that my spare Gator aid mix had split open and the powder was everywhere. What a mess and David was beside himself as well he should have been. My fault and I really felt badly about it. Gator aid mix does not get out of things easily, if at all.

Before I write more I should tell a little more about David Putnam, my climbing partner. We met in 1992 on a climb of a first assent of a 20,000 foot mountain in Buthan. And we have gone on most of our subsequent climbs together. He is the perfect partner. He went to Wesleyan, then on to law school and after a few years at a big New York firm "said the heck with it" and moved to Stowe, Vermont where he started a ski hat company. In the winters he was a ski instructor at Stowe Mountain.

David has a wild sense of humor, he is a very funny guy. He has a lawyer's talent for researching a subject and combines it with a desire to have all of the appropriate gear.

Consequently his side of our tent has lots of stuff and mine is just basic with "duct tape" holding my gear together. We have been called the "Odd Couple" but I would never climb without him.

So into the one duffel bag that will go to the high camp being carried by a porter, will be sleeping bag, pad, tooth brush, fleece top and bottoms and clean socks.

On my body when we start out from Khare camp, where we spend tomorrow night just before we get on the Mera La will be a medium poly bottom, medium and heavy poly top and my turtle fur hat. In my day pack will be the red down parka, Gore-Tex red Moonstone top and bottom, 1 liter water – no more gatorade for obvious reasons – trail mix, camera, one roll of toilet paper, climbing harness, crampons, ice ax, complete glove system of liner, Helly Hansen mitts, and Gore-Tex overmittes. I am very happy with all of my equipment. My gear feels right.

The times on my sheet that I did in Old Saybrook when I estimated the length of each day's trek have been very accurate so far. The altimeter continues to be consulted by everyone several times each day. Each night

after dinner, Adrian discusses the following day and starts by asking me to tell the group what the day will be like, how many hours, what kind of altitude gain, what kind of terrain, and how long we will be on the trail before we reach our camp site for the night. Amazingly the times I put together are right on the money. In fact, Adrian and have a contest to see who is closest in total travel time each day and my times are as close as his.

One last thing, Tagnag is still Maoist with a red flag atop a hill on the edge of town.

September 26
Khare
16,200 feet

It took about 3½ hours of steady uphill climbing to get here. We left at 8:00 and arrived at 11:30. It is 16,200' on Liz's altimeter. This is a very barren spot. Our tents are all in a row with David and mine at the end. There is another group here, the Russians. They are going to spend an extra day here, so we will be a day ahead them for the foreseeable future.

After a great lunch, we did our final packing. The next 2 days are it. Moving from here to High Camp will be a long day, probably 10 hours. We will start on scree for 2 hours, then move onto the Mera La glacier, roping up, with crampons, ice ax in uphill hand and ski pole in the other.

We should arrive at High Camp by dark, sleep 3 in a tent until 1 am or 2 am with most of our gear on. Our boots will be in our sleeping bag to keep them warm.

When we wake all we have to do is to put on our boots, our crampons and eat a little, at 19,400 you don't have much of an appetite and start climbing.

Hope to summit by 10 am to 12 noon and then get down to Honku camp by 5 pm or 6 pm. It will be a long day with only trail mix and 3 liters of water and 6 tubes of GU2.

It is now 5:10 pm and starting to get cold here. So far, I feel fine. I have acclimatized well and am moving well. I have a slight headache now, but I think that is induced by writing in a dark tent.

We spent the afternoon figuring out exactly

what to wear the next two days. I'm wearing light poly top and bottom, blue poly top, fleece top-Moonstone, and Red Gore-Tex suit.

I think I have a good chance but the next 2 days will be very hard going as we are from 16,200 feet to 19,400 to 21,500.

The team is in good shape except for Lissa who has a very bad cold, is a diabetic, and has a terrible sounding voice. On the plus side, she is very strong, lives in Aspen, and is determined. We talked a lot today climbing up here and I think she will make it.

Dan, 25 years old, is from Cortland, New York. He has upped his Diamox to 1,000 mg per day, the standard being 500 mg, and yet, he still has his headache. It is a concern, but he is also very strong.

Lynnette – Nettie the Australian – is a little over weight, which this climb should help her lose. After a pep talk from Adrian last night she did much better today.

The rest of the team includes Tim an Iron Man participant who is strong, but very undisciplined on the trail. He goes fast, slow, fast, slow. He is 49.

David is doing fine. He is over his cold and seems to be ready to give it a go.

Gay is in her mid to late 40's, looks like a dilettante, but in reality is very, very strong. She is inexperienced but she summited Cotopaxi, which is more than David or me.

We will learn our rope teams tonight at dinner.

I will not be writing for the next couple of days. I've done everything I could have done and I feel that I am the equal to everyone on the team. They have all been very complementary so I can't ask for anything more. Wish me luck.

September 27
Mera High Camp
19,400 feet

We left Khare at 7:00, walked for two hours until we got to the base, or nose, of the glacier. Nima had gone a little ahead and was on the glacier cutting steps so that the porters could get up onto the glacier itself. The face of the glacier was quite steep and the porters

only have tennis shoes, so without steps from Nima, they would just slip and slide.

As I looked up at the glacier and I saw that it levels off after the first ½ mile then it veers off to the right and out of sight. I sat on a rock, pulled out my crampons from my pack and strapped them on.

Our rope team for today is led by Adrian, followed by me and then Gay, David, Lissa and I think, Tim. We stand around for a few minutes and then head up and onto the face of the glacier.

The face is about a 45 degree angle but after about 600 yards we are up onto the glacier itself and moving quite nicely. We are moving up the glacier but it is nothing extreme.

We have the base of a mountain on our left and on our right is a flat snowfield. By 11:00 we are at the Mera La, the pass that leads down to where we will hopefully camp tomorrow night. We stop here and wait for the other rope team that is moving slower.

The porters leave us here and go down the Mera La to set up the next camp leaving only Nima, Kihlar the cook and a couple of

porters. They will go with us to set up high camp.

At the Mera La, it is a cold 40 degrees, overcast, with a slight wind. Altogether a not very nice place to sit and wait and to have a bite to eat, but what do you expect at 17,700.

All afternoon we continue on trudging up. It is very tiring as sometimes the sun is out and we get dehydrated. It is just one foot in front of another. Adrian says that high camp is up to the left behind some rocks but it sure looks a long way off to me.

I am very tired, in fact I am pooped if the truth be told. At 4:00 we round the rocks and find a small shelf with room for 3 tents and a little cave where Kihlar and a cook boy have set up a kitchen.

As we get to camp Gay says she'll bunk with David and me. Surprising, but later she confides that she felt the other tent would have been a "downer." How prophetic as we shall see.

This has been a very long day and people are moving very slowly if at all. Some are just sitting hoping that someone else will set up

their tent and settle the rest of camp. Even though I am shot, I try to keep moving.

We have a dinner of Shepard's stew at 5:00 pm and nobody says anything, some of us eat and others just look at their plates and do nothing. The team is not in very good shape, in fact most of the group looks terrible.

At dinner, David is wasted, Tim is shot, Nettie is just handing on, Dan has a massive altitude headache, and Lissa is starting to have a bad, bad chest cold. Gay is eating and I'm tired but not totally out of it.

As dinner ends Adrian announces the rope teams. Lissa, Gay and I will be with Jaime and David, Tim, and Nettie will be with Adrian. Our team is strong even though I am the only guy. The two girls are tough, Gay having climbed Cotopaxi with Jaime in February. Not bad for a mother of 4 girls ages 24, 22, 12 and 10.

As we get ready to crawl into our tents at 6 pm, there is a full moon rising to our East over a layer of clouds. It is a very cold, about 10 above. Our one concession to Gay is that we won't use our pee bottles tonight and as a result I see the full moon at least 4 times from 6 pm to midnight.

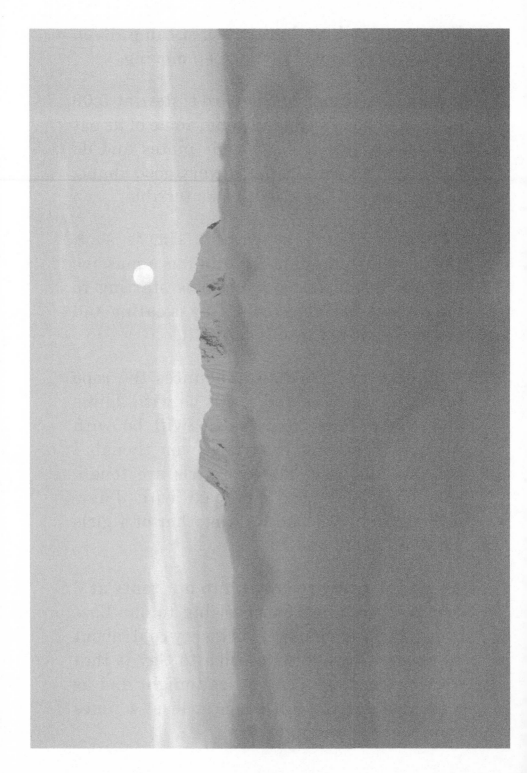

David goes to sleep in 10 seconds. And starts snoring very loudly and doing it continuously. Adrian is so concerned about David that he had taken me aside and asked that I wake David every hour to give him some fluids. I am to monitor his condition and if it deteriorates to wake Adrian.

On the other side of me Gay freshens herself with some sweet smelling stuff, puts in her ear plugs, takes an Ambien and off to sleep she goes. She moans or whimpers in her sleep so that the combination of sounds makes it impossible for me to catch even a wink.

I'm in the middle of a noise machine but I am treated to the bright moon during my visits outside the tent, which of course require me to at least partially dress to thwart the cold. On my last trip outside it has begun to snow, that doesn't portent of a nice climb!

September 28
Summit Day
21,247 feet

We are up at 1 and Adrian, after he has checked everyone out, announces new rope teams. David has had a remarkable

recovery. He is up and moving about. In fact, he is having a cup of coffee from Kihlar, and getting ready to go. Consequently he and I will climb with Adrian and Gay and Lissa will follow with Jaime.

The rest have had it. High Camp is their summit. They can't go any higher. Nima Sherpa will take them down to the Honku camp while we attempt to summit Mera. None of the 3, Tim, Nettie, and Dan as far as I can remember, even get out of their tent to wish us luck.

It sure was prophetic of Gay to choose our tent.

It is dark, cold and windy with spitting snow as we finish sorting out our gear and putting on our crampons. Nima helps me with mine. We stagger into our rope teams and off we go.

Our goal that we, David and I, have been thinking about and planning for during the past 2 years is just 2,000 vertical feet above us. It seems a long off in the dark especially after we had just done 3,000 vertical feet yesterday. Our head lamps don't penetrate very far, doing little beyond lighting up the

snow that is swirling around us.

We are on a breakable crust, so that with every footstep we sink into the snow up to the middle of our calves. That makes it not only slow going, but also very tiring.

Adrian had said that this would be the hardest day of our life and I'm beginning to see what he was talking about.

It is very much of a slog and very slow going. My mind is vacant except to focus on where I will place my foot. Very empty minded.

The 2 teams stay fairly close about 400 yards apart but at this altitude 400 yards is a long way. Slowly the climb becomes a death march. The 4 of us are shot from yesterday and recovery doesn't happen at this altitude. We are moving slowly, with Adrian's team being slightly faster than Jaime's. Frankly Jaime's pace is better suited to my old age.

Sometimes David asks for a blow, that is to stop and rest and sometimes I do. I try not to look up because the summit doesn't seem to get closer.

We stop one last time and Adrian say's that

it is not much further. Jaime's team comes up to us just as we are ready to start again and as I look at David, Lissa and Gay and it is clear that we are all shot! Just barely holding on.

Off we go at a snail's pace and then Adrian says "This is the Summit!" I look up at him and he is standing on a flat plateau. Several minutes later the other team arrives and we have all done what we had worked so hard to achieve.

Surprisingly I have no emotion, neither elation nor relief just "so this is it" – maybe I'm just too tired.

We take a few pictures and look at all the mountain tops below us. Yes in the distance are Everest, Lhotse and Nuputse and they seem to be below us. I may be the oldest ever to have summited Mera, not bad! It is 9 o'clock and we have been steadily climbing for 7 hours.

Adrian calls Nima on the radio, finds him still at high camp with the other three. He gives him the news we are on the top. As he looks down valley he tells Nima to quickly leave high camp as we can see weather coming in from below.

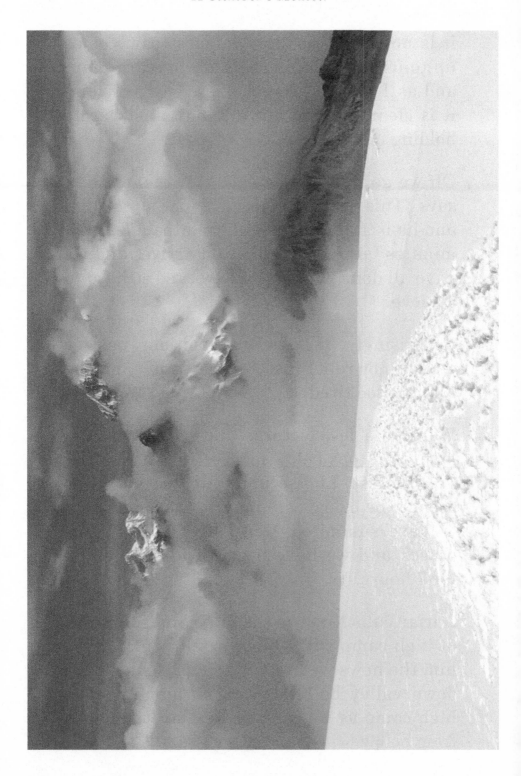

On summit day I wore medium poly top and bottom, heavy poly top, fleece top and bottom and my standby Moonstone Gore-Tex top and bottom. Gay said when she got to the top that during the night every time she looked up she saw this "red thing" and that kept her going. Glad I could help!

After 20 minutes on the summit the weather in the valley below is deteriorating so we start moving down off the summit.

What was breakable crust at 2 in the morning at 10 am is really breakable and we are sinking up close to the knee. It is awful. Post holing down, catching your feet, basically staggering off the peak. It is not so steep as to put one into a long fall but it is hard to keep on your feet.

Shortly we take off our crampons in hopes that will help – it doesn't. We reach high camp around 11. It is deserted except for the cook boy who has stayed behind to meet us and so he does with a thermos of hot lemon drink. He is very happy for us but we can only sit and drink. We don't talk much. We just sit and drink and in a few minutes it is time for us to continue on down to the Honku camp.

Descending to the Mera-La we are each on our own. Gay and I are together but don't say much, we just try to keep moving. Part way down we meet the Russians who are on their way up to high camp for their summit attempt tomorrow. We only talk for a moment to get their congratulations and for us to wish them luck.

It is a gradual decent down to the Mera-La on a white featureless snow field. We try to follow footprints, either those we made yesterday or those of the Russians. Nonetheless it is easy to get confused and at one point Gay and I are at the edge of a cliff before we realize that we should have gone more to the left. Adrian had said it would be the toughest day of our lives and he was right.

We reach Mera-La by 2 pm, where we rappel down a fixed line to the base of the glacier. This had been set up by the Sherpa's yesterday when they left us to go ahead and set up the camp we would be at tonight. We follow an up and trail for a couple of hours. We reach camp by 4. We are really dragging.

Our tent is set up in a lovely camp site next to a stream, but who cares. My systems seem as though they have all shut down. I am too

tired to even eat, but I try a little broth. Then I crawl into my sleeping bag, take a couple of Ibuprofen to counteract any aches and pains that I may develop and go off to sleep.

September 29
Tulu Danga
16,100 feet

We sleep in a little this morning and don't get moving in our tent until a few minutes before 7:00. The campsite is on a river bottom, very wide open and surrounded by wild country. There is nothing any direction but barren terrain. It looks like nobody has ever been here and with good reason for there is nothing to be found here. No trees, no animals no nothing.

By the time we are out of our tent, the porters are starting to break camp. They are ready to go since yesterday was a rest day for them. They are taking down the tents and putting their loads together as we grab a quick breakfast. By the time we get back to our tent the porters are waiting to tear it down. I quickly stuff things into my gear bag so that they can make up their load. I don't like to do things that way. I like to be

organized so that I know where all my gear is but today I'm moving slowly. I note that the other three who summited are also moving very slowly.

We get away by 8:00 but it is not a crisp departure, it is rather a slow stagger. The porters are all ahead of us except for a couple who have to break down the cook tent and get the last of our gear.

As we slowly hike no one is moving very well. Lissa is having a particularly hard time. She has had a bad chest cold and has a terrible cough. She gave it her all on summit day and is now exhausted. Nima is carrying her pack, but she still can hardly move. She is having trouble keeping up. Each time we take a break she just flops down and doesn't move until it is time to get up and going again.

She is a sweet girl with a degree from Georgetown and a Masters from Columbia in Fine Arts. She is trying to keep up with a professional guide, Adrian, who happens to be her fiancée.

It is a nice day. The trail has lot of ups and downs. It is a comfortable temperature, maybe 50 degrees. By lunch it has started to

rain again and it is a cold, cold rain.

We are starting to hike alongside the Hongku Khola – the Hongku river – a rough wild river. Several times we are right on the edge leaping from boulder to boulder, with just one on slip and you would be in over your head in a raging river – don't even think about the consequences.

This is pneumonia weather and the whole team sounds like they have it. Everyone is coughing from the cold rain and from the altitude. After one spends time at high altitude most everyone develops a bad cough. We begin to wonder about the money we have spent to be here to sound like a TB ward.

During one of the rest breaks I talk with Lissa and try to encourage her talking about how well she is doing and how she shouldn't use Adrian are her yardstick but rather be proud of what she has done.

The day ends alongside the Hongku Khola in an open plain. The entire country is wild with Everest, Lhotse, sometimes Makalu, Peak 41, and many other unnamed peaks on either side of the river. The trail is easy enough since we are all in good hiking shape.

One is constantly in awe of the remoteness of it all as we make camp at 16,100 feet.

I'm starting to feel better. I'm hydrating and starting to eat but it is hard to get all of my systems turned on.

We just counted up and we have lost 6 porters. They just up and leave their load and head for home.

They are afraid – all of the porters are – and they just say "to hell with it". They know it is just going to get worse and worse the further up the Hongu Khola valley we go. The only way out is over a high pass, either the Amphu Lapsha or the Mingbo La, which empties into Ama Dablam.

The porters loads are heavy, about 65 pounds, and they take many breaks during the day. They go fast and then they stop resting their load on a boulder rather than taking it off. Other times they take it completely off and have a smoke. They do concentrate and are expressionless, but when we pass each other we always smile and exchange "Namaste." They know each of us and who belongs to what, for at the end of each day our pack is always at the entrance of our tent.

We have dinner at 6:00 and are in our sleeping bag by 7:45. I am tired but starting to regain my strength.

Like always, I have at least a liter of water during the night when I wake up to use my pee bottle. In one end and out the other. As I was getting ready for dinner I could look way down the valley and see rain and snow clouds working their way slowly up toward our camp. By the time dinner was over it was cold and damp. It was however very nice in the tent and in my sleeping bag.

The last thing I did before I went to my tent was to try and use the satellite phone and call Old Saybrook. Kathie came through loud and clear. It was about 7:30 in the morning so I got her before she got out of bed. It was great to hear her voice, especially the relief in it. She should not worry, but I guess she does. It does make you homesick when you hear a voice from halfway around the world. Nice way to end the day.

After the call, I started to understand Rob Hall a little better. He died on Everest after calling his wife in New Zealand.

September 30
Hongku Khola Valley
17,050 feet

Up at 6:00 am with bed tea, eating at 7:00 and on the trail by 8:00. Today is a repeat of yesterday. Right along the Hongku Khola with Everest and Lhotse in front of us as we work our way up the valley.

The river valley is starting to widen out as the morning progresses. The trail is up and down, over and around boulders. Obviously, this is the debris from the river when it floods and carries all this glacial rock down from higher up in the valley. It is hard to imagine the power of this river until you think back to the Inkhu Khola of a week ago and how that river destroyed a whole village.

By lunch we are at the second of the Pach Pokhari sacred lakes. We are camped by 3:00 pm. This has been a nice day. We are at 17,356 feet, so there is a chill in the air.

The afternoon is a time for relaxation. Since we camped early, everyone is just hanging out. Adrian and Nima are bouldering and other people are throwing a Frisbee. The

porters are all having fun.

The afternoon snow squall looks like it is coming up the valley again right on schedule. I am definitely on the road to recovery as I feeling stronger every day.

Many on the team say they like to follow me because I have such a nice pace. That makes me feel good. I sure hope it lasts through Ima Tse, the Nepali name for Island Peak. My pace is as it always has been; steady, very measured and not real fast but not real slow.

October 1
Amphu Lapsha Base
18,200 feet

We are up and on our way by 8:00. We have been at an altitude of over 16,000 feet for more than 10 days so that we are now totally acclimatized.

Today we continue to move up the Hongku Khola valley. It is about ½ mile from side to side, with the rushing river on our right and towering peaks on our left, just one unnamed peak after another. In front of us is Makalu and beyond the river on our right is Peak 41.

In other words we are getting near the end of this valley with no way out except over a pass. On our left the pass is the Mingbo La which would take us down by Ama Dablam. Straight ahead is the Amphu Lapsha, which we will take to the base of Island Peak.

I now see why the porters are dropping out and heading back the way we came since neither of these passes looks inviting.

The trail we are on is very straight forward, a little up and down not severe but rather very pleasant. This morning the sacred lakes are on our right. By 11:00 we drop down and walk across the south shore on gravel and shortly the last of the sacred lakes is on our left.

By noon we stop for lunch and as usual Kihlar has made hot soup followed by grilled cheese sandwiches. He is fabulous in that we always have something hot for lunch. We eat around a blue tarp that is laid on the ground and the cook boy brings the food over from Kihlar's cooking area. The porters all stand over by Kihlar and grab something to eat. They rest a little while and then head off again. We normally take an hour break at lunch before heading out.

Today we are at the end of the Hongku
valley and to the East, behind our backs as
we eat is a small pass. It has been thought
that this pass may be the entrance to
Shan-gri-la. Yes the real Shan-gri-la! All
of the features that describe the entrance
to Shan-gri-la are just like this spot.

Right in front of us beyond the last lake is
the trail to the Amphu Lapsha and half way
up is the place for our high camp.

While having lunch, Jaime looked over at
Gay and said "What's that in your ear?" It
turned out to be one of her ear plugs that she
had used the night before summit day.

This was an eventful lunch for half way
through it Tim said "Hey that's my hat,"
and with that he rejoined our group. For the
last week even before Mera La he has been
disjointed and not mentally all together. He
had lost his hat over a week ago and now,
all of a sudden, he sees it! Obviously he has
been suffering from the altitude and mentally
slowed down. Now, in a flash, his mind has
cleared. Really one minute Tim was foggy
and the next he was sharp. Just like a switch
had been thrown.

Altitude does slow down your mental processes, which is why I always try to do everything in sequence. I put all my gear in the same place in the tent and put all my gear into my pack in the same way. That way I hope to not make many mistakes.

For the last 10 days, since before the Zair La, we have been followed by the team of Russians. They are young, in their 30's or 40's, and very strong. They never get ahead of us nor do they get very far behind us. They now say they are from Australia. We first saw them when they said they had to give the Maoist their guitar as a bribe. We have since learned that the guitar was returned to them the next day as none of the Maoists could play it.

Any way we only see the Russians from time to time as they have a very different pace than ours. They seem to be about a day behind us.

As we finish lunch we look up ahead and see our porters slowly moving toward high camp just below the Amphu Lapsha. The trail of loose scree is very steep.

We are now at 18,000 feet and moving slowly but steadily upwards. I am leading a group

and being careful with each foot plant. I am making short switchbacks, 3 steps in one direction and turning and going 3 short steps in the other direction. Always going up, if only to gain 2 or 3 inches with each step. The key is keep moving steadily, if slowly.

As the afternoon wears on it is getting cold and beginning to spit snow. This is not fun, this is work. It is cold and gray. We are in the middle of nowhere surrounded by huge mountains. I mention to Gay who is following close behind me that this is spectacular and that I am going to leave $5,000 in my will to pay for any of my grandchildren who want to come on this climb. I think this is something they should experience.

After several hours we reach the porters. They have established High Camp. So far, they have only put up a cook tent and they are all huddled inside it trying to stay warm. It is raw outside.

We crowd into the tent and wait for the snow squall to pass. After it passes we put up tents on very rough platforms.

We are spread out over a large area as there is no flat place for more than one tent in any

one spot. We are on scree. It is loose and steep so that a false step and it would be 1,500 feet down to the floor of the valley where we had lunch.

What do we see when we look down to our lunch site but the Russians! They have caught up with us. Our group is larger and moves daily at the pace geared to the slowest of our team, which would be Nettie the Australian girl.

It is cold, maybe 20 above with a brisk wind. David and I stay close to our tent as we sort our gear for tomorrow when we will go over the Amphu Lapsha. We are figuring out our clothing and getting our crampons and ice ax ready for the next challenge.

For the hike up the valley over the last 3 days we have only used our ski poles, now it is time for ice work. Nima, Adrian and Jaime are each trying to find the best route that will lead us out of the Hongu valley, over the Amphu Lapsha and into the valley of Island Peak. The regular way is on the "Wedding Cake" a tiered glacier but that does not seem practical due to its snow conditions. Finally, Nima finds a way over, which is right where the glacier and the rock join one another. It

is steep, he tells us, but it is the only way up and over the top from where we are.

From our tent platform we cannot take more that 2 or 3 steps before hitting loose scree and then you would fall at least ½ mile straight down. David says that we have skied stepper and he is probably right but then you have snow and metal edges, not loose scree.

Since our tent platform is so small, we are tent bound. Adrian comes over to our tent to give us the plan for the next 24 hours. Nima's route starts on rock and then joins a glacier. From the glacier we will go up the snow field which rises at about a 60 degrees angle using our jumars on the fixed ropes. Nima and the Russian sirdar will have set the rope.

We have supper in our tent. The cook boy brings by some soup and a cheese sandwich. We are to be up at 3:30 am and have bed tea at 4:00 and leave at 5:00, just at daylight. It is going to be a long day.

I plan my gear and lay it out in order so I can easily find and put it on in the dark and cold. On the bottom I will wear mid weight poly, fleece and Gore-Tex. On the top I'll wear mid

weight poly, heavy blue poly, fleece, and then my Gore-Tex.

This camp is 18,200 feet and it is desolate!

October 2
Over Amphu Lapsha
19,500 feet

So today it is up and over the Amphu Lapsha! 3:30 am comes early but we are moving on schedule at 5:00. As we struggle up and out of camp we can see the Russian head lamps down below at their camp.

We move well as a group, if a little ungainly, and slowly we work our way up the rocks to where they end and the snow glacier begins.

Here we stop, put on our crampons, tie into the fixed rope and jumar up the first pitch. It goes up straight and then veers to the right before it flattens out.

A jumar is a climbing tool that is attached to a fixed rope and aids one in climbing by providing security. The jumar is a cam device that slides up the rope but cannot slide down, so a climber is always attached to something

fixed by continually sliding the jumar up the rope.

Mixed in with the climbers are the porters and they need help maneuvering with their loads. Our group is about 35 people – guides, climbers, porters and so we move slowly, but steadily.

It takes time to tie people in, and then to climb.

We are now at 19,000 feet. Several of the climbers are sick. Dan when over 16,000 feet gets a pounding headache. He just cannot acclimatize. Nettie has a bad cold, is overweight, and slow – not a very good combination. I try to tie in behind Gay as she moves at a good pace for me.

There are many transitions on the ice, meaning that we have to move past a place where an ice screw is securing the fixed rope. At those spots we always put in a backup first. We do that by placing a carabineer above the transition, then removing our jumar and placing it above the transition. That way we are always protected by the carabineer if we slip. But making all the transitions for all those people takes time. A long time.

We reach the end of the flat section and are now at the base of the 60 degree snow field that goes up for several pitches, about 400 feet, to the top of the Amphu Lapsha.

As we rest we are looking right down the valley where we have spent the last 4 days.

It is a place with total exposure. We are on a small ledge with our feet pointing out and beyond our feet is nothing but air.

To get off this ledge we have to swing out and scramble up a rock face for about 20 feet until we reach the snow. One bad step here and it is 3,000 feet down. Trust your rope, don't look down and concentrate.

When it is my turn, I swing to the left, my crampons clang on the rock, making sparks, and I finally reach the ice. Whew! I don't want to do that again.

I am behind several porters and the one directly in front of me has on tennis shoes! His legs are shaking and he can't seem to move.

There are rudimentary steps cut into the ice but he can't place his foot into the next one

and he is slipping backwards into me. He has both hands on the rope and it is slowly slipping through his hands. To stop him from taking several of us down with him, last year 3 porters right here did fall down, I put my head into his load. That takes the weight of his load off of him and on to me.

Since I have on crampons I am secure but even so my legs are starting to shake under this added strain. After a minute, he starts to regain his strength and begins to move. This is not fun.

The porters just ahead of me keep pulling the fixed rope to the left toward the rocks and I keep trying to go to the right to stay on the ice. The porters keep trying to find the steps cut into the ice by Nima but often there are not any and then they go down onto their knees and sort of crawl. This is a very stressful time and I now realize why those porters abandoned the climb days ago rather than face this effort.

Slowly I keep moving up and the ice starts to flatten out. Finally I am at the end of the last pitch. That's it, the top.

But I am not alone for I see people off to my

left about 30 yards away and I move over towards them. David is behind me and he is helping Nettie. He tells me later that he has been doing the same thing for her that I did for the porter in front of me.

As I join the group I look out and realize that we are now looking down on the valley of Island Peak or as known in Nepal, Imja Khola. Wow, there is the Lhotse face and below it is Island Peak our next climb.

Within this group of 4 or 5, I notice a porter that is unfamiliar and then I see one of the Russians. It seems that the two groups have gotten interconnected. Since our team moves more slowly than the other group they have caught up with us.

We are gathered at the top of an ice face waiting our turn to rappel down a fixed rope. It is about 150 feet before it flattens out onto a space about 10 feet by 20 feet. The rappel is very steep so I tie in at the top and double check my protection before I head down when it is clear for me to go. Only one person at a time can be on the rope.

Shortly after I get to the flat spot where most of our team has congregated David and Nettie

appear. David and I hang off to the side and he regales me with his tale of getting Nettie over the top.

As David tells the Nettie saga we can hear the porters off to our left. They are lowering their loads over a cliff and then they will go down unencumbered and collect them. It is chaos as some of the loads are not well secured and they go careening down the mountain until they stop. The porters don't care how far down the loads go. Actually the further the loads go, the shorter distance to the camp site. Whether our gear gets busted or not is of no concern of theirs. They are happy to be over the Amphu Lapsha and can't wait to get to the valley floor.

We are still waiting on the flat spot.
It has gotten crowded since the Russians and their porters have caught up with us. Adrian Nima and Jaime are fixing a rope about 50 feet off to our right. It is another 200 foot ice face. It is a steep face and access to it is along a very narrow scree path maybe 8 inches wide. I remark to David that this is no walk in the park.

At that very instance we hear a commotion where the ropes are being fixed. The

commotion is caused by Nima. He has slipped, unroped and gone down the ice face. He has landed on some rocks and ice several hundred feet below the end of the ice face.

He is dead.

It is very hard to process what has happened. Each of us is numb. Nettie is sobbing. Nima has been particularly close to her, always helping her, since she was always so far behind the rest of us.

We are all just stunned. Your mind doesn't process things like this very well at sea level and at 18,000 feet it is just that much more difficult to comprehend what has happened.

Nima's fall is a classic high altitude accident. A little error here and a little error there and all of a sudden you have a critical mass and something terrible happens. In this case, Nima was rushing. He was not roped up because he was hurrying to set up the fixed rope. He was anxious because of the crowd of people. There were all the Russians, their porters, his clients and his porters. In other words too many people stuffed into a small space. He just slipped and was gone. Adrian

got down to him quickly but he had died instantly.

But Adrian has to keep going, he has all these climbers and porters to get off of the Amphu Lapsha. Between Adrian, Lissa, and Jaime the rope gets set and everyone goes down the ice face.

Lissa is at top checking out that everyone is tied in properly and Jaime at the bottom, getting people off and on down the trail. It is important to keep moving.

After we have moved for 15 or 20 minutes beyond the terminus of the fixed rope, we stop and Adrian tells us exactly what has actually happened. As Adrian moves by me, he stops for a moment and is shaking as he leans against me and quietly sobs. After a minute he gets it together. Before we start to continue down I ask that we all say a prayer for Nima's soul.

It is time to move on and get off the mountain. It is now the middle of the afternoon. It is cold, gray and overcast. We are going down a scree slope, just sort of putting one foot in front of the other. The whole team is quiet and lost in their own thoughts.

Two thousand feet down, we can see the valley floor and we can't wait to get there. There is a small glacial lake at our camp site and on the other side of the lake is a team of Australians. They have come up from Chungkung and are going to go over the Amphu Lapsha tomorrow.

As we reach our camp, the tents are set up on the scree and they are scattered around quite haphazardly. The porters are disorganized and upset. They just want out. This is a remote, cold, damp and forlorn camp.

After David and I find our tent, we drop our packs, and I say to myself as I step out of my climbing harness "Well, that's the last time I will wear this!" I figure my climbing days are over. Obviously, we won't climb Island Peak and that ends the big mountains for me. A death on Denali several years ago on a team adjacent to mine, and now Nima. That is enough for me. No sense in pushing my luck.

David and I wander over to the dining tent. It is dark as dusk is settling in. Kihlar is trying to make soup. Adrian is trying to reach Katmandu to report what has happened. Shortly he sticks his head into the dining tent to report that he has made contact and

that the plan is for the team to leave in the morning for Chungkung with Kihlar in the lead. We are to go ahead and set up camp in the yard of the Ama Dablam tea house in Chungkung.

Adrian, Jaime, Endow and Pemba, along with 8 porters, are to go up and try to get Nima's body. If they are successful the porters will carry him down.

It is expected that Nima's body will go to Namche Bazaar where his wife and young son are staying.

Nima will be missed. He was a wonderful Sherpa, guide, and sirdar. He was a perfect man in the mountains.

Island Peak, crowded as it is with several other climbing teams and with the limited skills of this group is not going to be part of our Nepal climbing adventure. In fact as I said when I got off Amphu Lapsha and took off my harness "that's that."

The interesting thing is that Adrian is part of the new generation of guides. He is really terrific, very safety conscious, like no one I have ever climbed with before. He is a fanatic

for safety and backup, and yet accidents do happen in this environment. One contributing factor is that there are more less experienced people coming to the mountains, so the guides are working harder and harder to accommodate the limited skills.

October 3
Chungkung
15,700 feet

The cook boy is at the tent at 6:00 with "bed tea," we have breakfast at 7:00 and are on the trail by 8:00. We are being led by Kihlar and get to Chungkung by 12:30 after a spectacular hike out.

During the night, we had 3 or 4 inches of new, fresh, wet snow. There is very low visibility so that we cannot even see Amphu Lapsha. The Australians will not have much fun going up and over the pass today and it is doubtful that Adrian will be able to find Nima's body, much less get him out.

As we descend from our camp and begin hiking toward Chungkung, Island Peak and Nuptse come into view. On our left is the Amphu Lapsha in the distance and close by are some spectacular unnamed peaks, with

a wonderful glacial lake at their base. It has gotten warmer, the snow has melted and the trail is open and level.

To our right is a roaring river that we will have to cross in order to get to Chungkung. Kihlar tries to make the crossing easy for the team and ends up standing in the frigid river up to his thigh for 20 minutes as he helps people get across. David and I hang back and watch, knowing that when our turn comes we will just leap from boulder to boulder and take Kihlar out of his misery. We are somewhat successful but do slip in near the far side. Yes, the water is cold!

The team spreads out on this last section before the tea house and David and I remark to one another on how fit we are, how this is the best we have ever been at this stage in a climb. Little did we know.

At the Ama Dablam tea house, we talk with 2 groups that are going toward Island Peak. So far this season no one has summited Island Peak due to a large crevice that has opened up. To cross it you would need 2 ladders and they are not to be found in Chungkung – a place with a tea house and a couple of small seasonal stone Shepard huts.

Since we cannot climb Island Peak we need to come up with an alternative plan. I'm inclined to go toward Gorek Shep and Everest Base Camp and come back here in week. This is the place where we are to be resupplied for the balance of our adventure. When we left Lukla we only took enough food and other supplies to get us up and over the Amphu Lapsha. The rest of our food will be coming up from Lukla through Namche Bazaar and here to Chungkung.

It is now 5:30 pm. In the tea house a light has just been turned on and a yak dung fire has been made in the stove. I have spent the afternoon at a table getting my journal up to date.

Adrian and Pemba Sherpa appear at the tea house and say "Everything O.K. We got Nima."

October 4
Periche
14,200 feet

It's 3 AM and I wake feeling diarrhea coming on... and coming on right now. I feel faint. In fact, I feel so weak that I can't get out of my

sleeping bag so I call out to David "help." He
rolls over and comments "it's too late."

With that he drags me out of my bag and out
of the tent. He says that I've already started
having diarrhea. He gets me 2 steps out of
the tent and I collapse onto the ground on
all 4's. David says "you're passing blood and
I'm going to wake Adrian." I'm on all 4's, in
a doggie position, firing away, head on the
ground, butt raised and I'm out of control – I
can't stop.

It is cold, maybe 30 degrees, and I am naked
except for a mid poly top. Adrian comes,
takes one look and goes to wake Kihlar to
heat water and gets some towels to clean up
the mess.

After half an hour the diarrhea slows down
and David starts to clean me up. What a job
he has but he does it with his usual good
humor. He uses the warm water and towels
and every time he gets close to being done I
fool him and have another attack.

Finally I stop and I am clean, but now I'm
cold. David and Adrian bundle me up and
carry me inside the tea house where they
lay me on a bench. The rest of the night I

rest and someone is always with me, either David, Adrian or Jaime. Adrian has given me Cipro and lomotal and the combination seems to work.

At sunrise they move me to a private room with a cot and Adrian asks if I want to fly out at 10 am with Nima's body. No, I say that I would prefer to hike down to the health post at Periche, which is several thousand feet lower in altitude and several kilometers away. The health post serves Everest and the upper Khumbu region.

Adrian agrees and we plan to start at 10:30 am or 11. I dress, but I am very weak. I sit outside in the courtyard of the tea house and continue to feel progressively weaker.

Our plan is for Adrian and Lissa to go with me and I'll be helped by Pemba Sherpa and Endow. Unfortunately, as I stand up, I take 3 steps and fall to the ground.

Now to plan B. It is decided that the only way to get me down is to build a litter and enlist 8 porters plus Pemba and Endow to carry me down to Periche. So, the litter is built. It made up of 2 poles, each about 10 feet long and with a 4 foot cross piece near each end.

There is a blanket covering the frame. I'm tied in to this. Actually ropes are wrapped around and around and around me so that not only can I not fall out, I can't move.

Off we go down the steep trail. We move at a steady pace and from time to time either Lissa or Adrian come close to me and ask how I'm doing. My feet are facing downhill and I can just see the mountains that tower up around us. The porters alternate as they get tired. One will make what sounds to me like a grunting sound, and a porter will move in and take his place. This is done on the fly. We cross numerous streams and finally after one last very, very steep decent we reach the health post.

The health post at Periche is operated by the Himalayan Rescue Association, an organization founded by Sir Edmund Hillary. It is staffed by volunteers and funded by contributions. Dr. Linda Johannson is from British Columbia and Dr. Mike Grocert is from London. They will spend 3 to 4 months at Periche.

Dr. Linda and Dr. Mike greet me outside. Dr. Linda takes one brief look at me and says "We have to get you out by helicopter." I

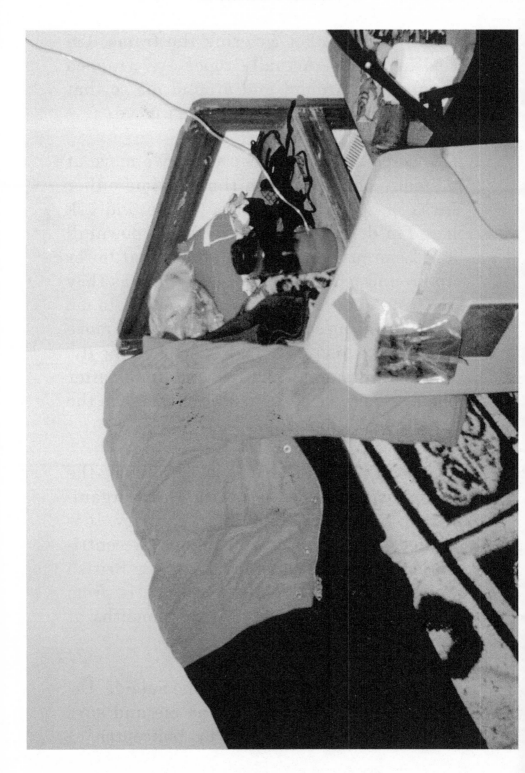

object and say I'll hike out with my friends tomorrow. With that they bundle me onto a bunk, begin IVs and put an oxygen mask over my face. I'm really weak but at least I'm now in the hands of a couple of doctors.

After being settled, I ask Dr. Linda to call Kathie. I'm really too weak to talk on the Satellite phone and my emotions are too ragged. She gives Kathie the news as to where I am, what is going on, and what they plan to do. Dr. Linda says "Not to worry".

Later, Dr. Linda sits on the edge of my bunk and asks "Do you want extreme measures done?" I reply that I have a living will. She asks again. I repeat that I have a living will. She asks a third time and this time I reply that I would like measures taken as long as they don't leave me as a vegetable. That seems to satisfy her. With that settled I drift off to sleep attached to an IV and oxygen.

October 5
Periche Health Post
14,200 feet

I wake early after a restless night and get ready for the helicopter. Yes, Dr. Linda

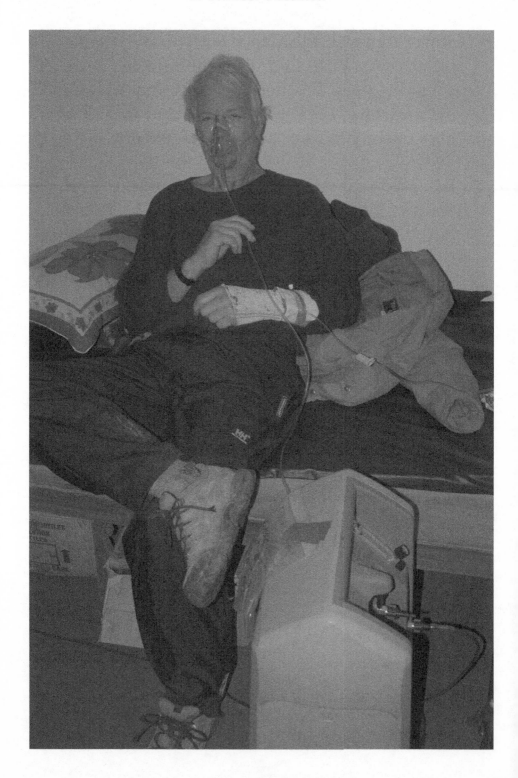

prevailed. I feel fairly weak, but OK. The weather is bad between Kathmandu and Lukla so the helicopter has turned back.

Around 11 am the team arrives from Chungkung and I start to feel weaker even though I have had noodle soup with Dr. Mike and Dr. Linda at coffee break time. I pass some more blood and stay in my bunk hooked up to IV and oxygen.

At 4 pm, I ask Mike for help to go to the toilet. He goes with me as he wants to see the color I am passing. I go, he checks the color and the next thing I remember I am on the floor with Adrian lifting my feet high into the air and Mike and Linda at my chest. I had passed out. They carry me back to my bunk and hook me up again to the IVs and place the oxygen mask over my mouth.

Now I can hear Dr. Linda on the satellite phone really pressing for a helicopter, and I mean urgently asking for it to come ASAP. Nothing can fly due to the weather. Also Periche is at 17,000 feet and that is near the upper operating limit of the helicopter.

I'm obviously getting weaker. Furthermore I know that Dr. Mike and Dr. Linda are getting concerned.

As I lay there all hooked up and getting weaker by the hour I start to reflect on the fact that I've had a good life and that this might not be the worst place from which to leave this earth. After all, I'm surrounded by friends and by beautiful peaks like Ama Dablam and Everest.

Bleeding to death is painless as you just get weaker and weaker and then drift off. I get some visits from the team but they are brief as I don't have much energy to talk. The team is on a rest day which I am sure is appreciated by the porters if no one else.

In the evening, Dr. Mike stops in and says the best weather window is early in the morning between 6 to 7 AM tomorrow and that he will accompany me to Katmandu in the helicopter. He gives me a "yak bell" and tells me to ring it if I need anything during the night. I don't sleep well and I do ring the bell twice.

October 6
Nordic International Hospital, Kathmandu

It is 6 am and the helicopter is coming. As the porters carry me out of the health post

Dr. Linda gives me a bill and in exchange I ask for a Himalayan Rescue Association Tee shirt. The porters hurry me to the landing area and the helicopter comes swooping in, touches down and throws open the door. I am tossed into the back onto the floor and I am followed in by Dr. Mike. Lettie tries to follow but is pushed out by the pilot who slams the door.

In the 45 seconds that the helicopter has been on the ground the engine has been roaring. As soon as that door slams shuts we are moving forward and lifting off.

We swoop down the river valley, over Namche Bazaar and on towards Lukla. At Lukla we land right next to the terminal from which we had departed on our climb several weeks ago. I sit on the curb by the gate while our pilot loads fuel into the helicopter and looks for his co-pilot.

The only way for the helicopter to get to the health post at Periche was to go by way of Lukla where they could lighten the craft by getting rid of the excess fuel and the co-pilot. That is why the pick up at Periche was so fast and why the extra weight of Lettie was not allowed.

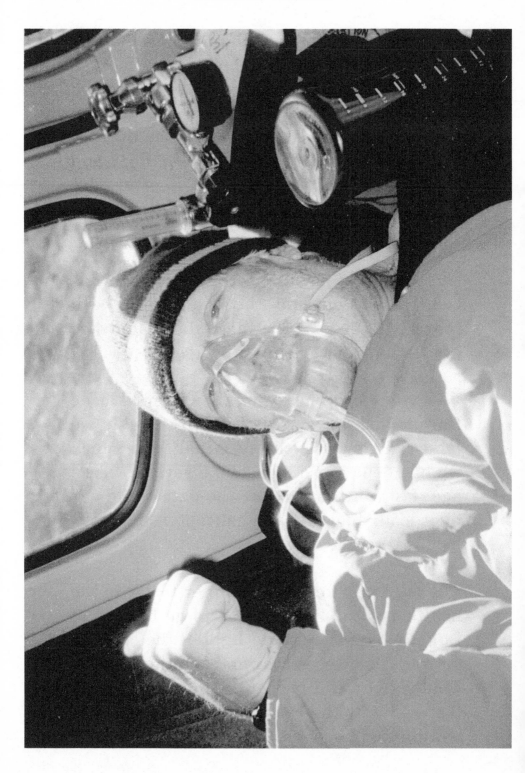

At this lower altitude of Lukla I am already feeling stronger.

We fly on to Katmandu, which is an hour of fabulous sights and the airport comes into view. We land, I take one step and am placed into a waiting ambulance for a siren ringing ride to the hospital. At one point in the ride Dr. Mike asks the driver to slow down because he is scared of the careening of the ambulance.

We arrive at the hospital and I am whisked into the emergency room. I am now under the care of Nepalese doctors. The next few hours are a blur of tests and then I am wheeled to my room. It dawns on me that I am getting special treatment at Norvic Hospital as my room is a suite; a bedroom, a bath and a living room. I have asked Dr. Mike to be my "mouthpiece" in talking to the Nepalese doctors.

In mid-afternoon I am aware of a lot of bustle outside my door and then in comes a doctor followed by a second doctor and 3 nurses. Obviously this is the head man. Every word he says is taken down by one of the nurses and the junior doctor nods his head a lot.

After several minutes of examining me the

Hematology

NHCC No	COO		Reg No	4853
Name	Mr Charlie Berry		Date	6th Oct, 2004
Age/Sex	69/M		Consultant	
Lab No	127/20		Referred By	
Bed No	201		IPD/OPD No	Emergency

BLOOD EXAMINATION REPORT

TESTS			REFERENCE RANGE
Hb	4.9	gm%	M 13-17, F 12-15
PCV	15	%	M 40-50, F 36-46
Platelets	198000	/cmm	150000-400000/cmm
WBC (TLC)	3700	/cmm	4,000 - 10,000 /cmm
WBC (DLC) :			
Neutrophils	57		40-80%
Lymphocytes	41		20-40%
Monocytes	-		2-10%
Eosinophils	1		1-6%
Basophils	1		<1-2%
ESR	4mm in 1st hour		M.0-10 mm F.0-20mm
Bleeding time	2min30 sec		2 –7 min
Clotting time	9min 30sec		5 - 11 min
Prothrombin Time Test	15sec		
Control	15sec		
INR	1.0		2 - 4
BLOOD GROUPING :	ABO : 'O'		Rh. D : Negative

Dr. RAJESH PANTH
MD PATH (NMC#1048)

P.O. Box 14126, Thapathali, Kathmandu, Nepal
Tel : (+977-1) 4258554, Fax (+977-1) 4219668, E-mail: hosp@norvic.wlink.com.np
An ISO 9001:2000 Certified Pathologist

chief doctor looks me straight in the eye and says "You are a very lucky man, you've been blessed with a new life, whether you believe that or not, you could have gone into shock and....."

I learn later that the initial blood test at the hospital showed my hemoglobin count to be a "4" which is why his remark was so direct. The hospital urgently searches Kathmandu for "O" negative blood which they finally find, but which, after talking with Dr. Mike, I politely refuse.

It is determined that the cause of my gastrointestinal bleeding is the several Ibuprofen that I took at the end of summit day just before I had gone to sleep. It says on the label to take with food. I didn't, and over the course of 5 days the Ibuprofen slowly perforated my stomach. Dr. Mike says he has seen 5 cases like this... high altitude and Ibuprofen causing GI bleeding.

October 7, 8, and 9
Norvic International Hospital, Kathmandu

I am in the hospital and the last several days have gone by quickly as I have been slowly

NORVIC - ESCORTS INTERNATIONAL HOSPITAL

BLOOD REQUISITION, REPORT, CROSS-MATCH & TRANSFUSION RECORD

Name: MR CHARLIE BERRY   Age/Sex: 69/M   NORES No.: _____   Dept: _____

Consultant: Dr Mohean khoturey / Dr R pande   Bed No.: _____ OPD/IPD No.: _____ Date: 2004/10/06

Provisional Diagnosis & Clinical Details: GI Bleed with Anaemia.

| EXAMINATION REQUESTED | ABO Blood Group | 'O' | BH Blood Group | -ve | Date Required 2004/10/06 |

AMOUNT REQUIRED   DATE AND HOUR WANTED URGENT NOW

PREVIOUSLY TRANSFUSION
YES ☐
NO ☑
If Yes, Number of times _____

REACTION TO PREVIOUS TRANSFUSION
Blood Yes ☐ No ☐
Plasma Yes ☐ No ☐ X

IF PATIENT IS FEMALE, IS THERE HISTORY OF
Still Birth Yes ☐ No ☐
Erythroblastosis Yes ☐ No ☐
Miscarriage Yes ☐ No ☐

Remarks and Comments of Requesting Doctor

"O" "NEGATIVE" BLOOD

Date	Subsequent Requests	Signature of Physician
7/10/06	IV O of fresh whole blood).	2004/10/06

CROSS-MATCH AND BLOOD BANK ISSUES

Date	B.B. No.	Cross match done by Signature	Checked by (Signature)	Quality of blood Issued	cDate	Time	Initials
20.6.06	1761	compatible			20.6		
	1763				20.6		

Signature of Doctor with date

If Hemolytic Rectionis suspected blood from opp arm & urine shoould be examined immediately

F:IPD:21/Rev.02/01.02.03

getting better. I have been hooked up to three IVs and I have been sleeping a lot. I have had phone calls from Kathie and the girls from the states and that is only thing that breaks the boredom.

I have had blood tests every day and on October 7th the hemoglobin had gotten up to a 6. That makes the doctors happy as it shows improvement. They say I can be discharged when the Hb gets to 9.

On October 7th I was wheeled out of my room and down to the Endoscopy unit for an exam. No one told me this was going to take place and it was a shock. They asked me to open my mouth and then they inserted a tube down my throat and into my stomach. They took pictures as it went all the way down to my stomach and Dr. Mike and the specialist maintained a continuous dialogue. Most of their conversation was unintelligible but at one point I heard Dr. Mike say "There's the Schertz ring" in the esophagus. I recognized that name since it was named for Ralph's partner in Boston.

All that time I'm gagging as they have given me no anesthesia. Just "Keep your mouth open and bite on the hollow tube."

NORVIC-ESCORTS
International Hospital

<u>**Endoscopy unit**</u>
<u>**Digestive Disease Centre**</u>

UPPER G. I. ENDOSCOPY

NHCC No		Reg. No	338
Name	Mr. Charlie Berry	Date	7th October, 2004
Age/Sex	69/M	Refered By	Prof. Mahesh Khakurel
Address			
Phone No.		Endoscopist	Dr. P. K. Shrestha
IPD /OPD No		Bed No	201

<u>**Indication**</u> : Epigastric pain

<u>**Medication**</u> : 2% Xylocaine spray over the pharynx and pyriform fossa.

<u>**Findings**</u> :

1. <u>Oral cavity, pharynx and larynx</u> : Normal.

2. <u>Oesophagus</u> :

> Upper – normal
> Middle – normal
> Lower – circumferancial stricture present. No reflux seen.
> E-G Junction – normal, No hiatus hernia

3. <u>Stomach</u> :

> Fundus – normal
> Body – normal gastric folds normal
> Antrum – erosions around the p-ring but no bleeding
> P-ring- normal

4. <u>Duodenum</u> :
> Bulb – erosions +, oedema on anterior wall present but no bleeding
> 2ND part – normal
> Papilla – normal

IMPRESSION :   LOWER OESOPHAGEAL STRICTURE
               GASTRO – DUODENITIS

Signature

Dr. Pradeep K. Shrestha

The hospital does not supply meals. They provide a menu from a local take out restaurant from which the patients may order. For every lunch and dinner I have had chicken fried rice.

I took my first shower in two weeks and I feel clean although I still look a little dirty.

I went for a 10 minute walk in the halls and I am starting to feel stronger.

This hospital is very quiet. I'm in the private patient wing and there are only a few rooms occupied.

My primary doctor is very elegant. He is the King of Nepal's personal physician. He wears Yves St Laurent monogram shirts, YSL ties and nicely tailored slacks. He comes by every morning at 7 am and again before he leaves at 7 pm. He is always trailed by a group of 3 or 4, including another doctor and several nurses. He is very professional and very much a decision maker.

My blood pressure is taken at least 5 or 6 times a day, both lying down and then standing up. And of course my blood is drawn daily. There are 3 points of access in my arm so they have

Norvic-Escorts
International Hospital

नर्भिक एस्कर्ट्स् इन्टरनेशनल हस्पीटल

DISCHARGE SUMMARY

Name: Mr.Charlie Berry	AGE/SEX: 69/M	BED NO : 112
NHCC NO: 24548	IPD NO : 2082	WARD: Deluxe
ADMIT DATE : 06 /10/04	DISCHARGE DATE: 10/10/04	
CONSULTANT : Dr.R.Pande/Dr.M.Khakurel		

FINAL DIAGNOSIS:

NSAID INDUCED UGI BLEED
GASTRODUODENITIS
LOWER OESOPHAGEAL STRICTURE

CLINICAL NOTES:

Mr.Berry 69yr/M,non smoker was trekking at a height of 6000mt.He had back pain and so was taking T.Brufen around 2-3 tabs/day for around 3 days.Then he experienced fresh bleeding PR for last 3 days,total 6-7 episodes.He was managed in Pheriche HRA with IV fluids,IV Ranitidine,C.Omeprazole.Then he experienced some burning retrosternal discomfort and also had 1 episode of Syncopal attack.He then was reffered to us for further management.

PHYSICAL EXAMINATION

G.C	fair	CHEST	B/L clear
PULSE	64/min	CVS	S1+S2+M0
BP	120/80 mm Hg	P/A	soft, tender, no organomegaly
TEMP	Afebrile	CNS	intact
JA++LCCyOD			

INVESTIGATIONS

ALL REPORTS ENCLOSED
UGI Endoscopy[07.10.04] Lower oesophageal stricture,Gastroduodenitis.

F:IPD:66/Rev.00/01.08.04

P.O. Box: 14126, Thapathali, Kathmandu, Nepal., Tel. : 4258554, Fax : (+977-1) 4219686

3 IVs going all time.

The nurses work 7 pm to 7 am several days in a row, then a day off, then 7 am to 7 pm for several days. All are young 21 or 22 and well trained. I have a new room on ward that is the size of my office with an adjoining bath, a pink and gray bed, and a TV on a stand. They change my sheets every day, and now I get new PJs every day. For my shower, an orderly stands in the doorway ready to assist.

Other than Dr. Mike the only visitor I have had has been the hospital CFO, who wants to know how they will be paid. I told him I had insurance, gave him the Blue Cross telephone number in New Haven that Amy had gotten for me and he called them.

Of course he had to make the call at midnight Kathmandu time and he reported that Blue Cross would not directly reimburse him. We agreed that I would put the bill on my Visa Card and I asked Kathie during one of our telephone calls to so advise Visa.

As I was being discharged from the hospital several days later I was presented with a bill for 99,000 Nepali rupees. As I was getting into a cab to go to my guesthouse who hops

NORVIC
Norvic-Escorts
International Hospital

नर्भिक एस्कर्टस् इन्टरनेशनल हस्पीटल

DISCHARGE SUMMARY

COURSE IN THE HOSPITAL:

He was admitted for further evaluation and management.All relevant investigations were done which revealed Hb:6.2%,FOBT +ve.UGI Endoscopy was done which revealed Lower oesophageal stricture,Gastroduodenitis.He was treated with IV fluids,IV Ranitidine.Blood transfusion was planned but the patient refused.So he is being treated with Iron supplement and Pantoprazole.His general condition is good.He walks around.initially he had postural hypotension which has resolved now.He is stable and is being discharged with following advice.

ADVICE ON DISCHARGE:

Medications:

T.Ferrofolic 1 Cap. OD X ....months. *once a day after meal.*

T.Pantop 40mg BD *twice a day morning a.f evening*

T.Alprax 0.25mg SOS at HS *– if necessary.*

ADVICE: Avoid exertion.

F/U in Dr R.Pande's OPD on *14th Oct* at *5:PM with Hb/PCV .*

F/UP in Dr.M.Khakurel's OPD on..........at........ *5:30 PM thsday*
Haemoglobin + PCV
5 PM thsday

_____   *mahuh ku...*   _____

Dr.R.Pande   Prof.M.Khakurel   Dr.Saroj Dhakal
Cons.Physician   Con.Surgeon   Med.Officer

F:IPD:66/Rev.00/01.08.04

P.O. Box: 14126, Thapathali, Kathmandu, Nepal., Tel. : 4258554, Fax : (+977-1) 4219686
E-mail : heart@norvic.wlink.com.np Website : www.norvichospital.com

~ 144 ~

into the front seat of the taxi but the CFO! He wants my Visa card number.

All the way to the guest house I try to convert 99,000 Nepali rupees into $ and every time I do it, it comes out the same. It must be wrong for it includes my room, the doctors, the Endoscopic exam, and it comes to $1,700.00 US.

And that is the end of the story.

EPILOGUE

I spend the next few days at the guest house waiting for the rest of the team to arrive from the Khumbu.

After a final dinner with all of the team including Adrian, Jaime, Endow Sherpa and Pemba Sherpa we depart Kathmandu for our trip home.

David and I go to Bangkok where we are joined by Kathie who flies in from the states. She and I continue with the plans we had made months ago of spending 3 weeks travelling around Thailand and Cambodia.

Fortunately we had planned on spending the first week in a beach front cabin in KoLanta. There I start to gain some of the 20 pounds I had lost. Also the beautiful sun started to rid me of my gray pallor.

To date I have not climbed another big mountain but I am sustained by the 30 years of great memories.

The question always comes up "Why." Why

climb the big mountains as I have done over the last 30 years when it is obvious from this story that to be on an expedition takes a big physical toll.

I started climbing because of the challenge, the same kind of drive that got me into running marathons. These activities require focus and training. Nothing else matters, not the college you went to nor the title you have on your office door. Nothing, but your ability to put one foot in front of the other.

Over time, however, I realized that I was gaining as much from the interchange with the locals as I was from the accomplishment of reaching the summit. Thus experiencing the indigenous people and their culture has become the major factor in my continuing to climb.

I should conclude with a few comments about the lessons I've learned over those years of climbing the big mountains.

1. Climbing is more mental than physical.

2. A good climbing partner is essential, to give you security on the rope as well as encouragement when your spirits are flagging.

3. Always prepare by training hard. You cannot rush acclimatization. You can only go high after you have spent time adjusting to the altitude and the resultant decrease in oxygen.

I hope you have enjoyed this story. As I have read this manuscript before I send it to the publisher, 7 years have elapsed since those 3 weeks in 2004. Those events however are still so fresh in my mind that they could have taken place just last month.

POSTSCRIPT

In the summer of 2012 during my 77th year I was invited by my daughter Liz to join her and her three sons on a climb of Kilimanjaro, at 19,500 feet, the highest mountain Africa.

It was arduous but at the end of 6 days, they reached the absolute summit and I stopped just short of that at Stella Point. Since Tanzania controls the mountain and forces climbers along at a pace that does not permit proper acclimatization, I was satisfied with reaching Stella Point, 150 feet below the top. And this is the end of the climbing story for as I reached the bottom of Kilimanjaro I gave most of my climbing gear to our Tanzanian guides and porters.

To each of my grandchildren I have left a framed picture of one of my climbs so if you are ever curious about some of the other mountains I have been on contact one of them.